Greetings, big rigs!

MARVELS VEHICLES 29

BIG RIGS

QUINN M. ARNOLD

CREATIVE EDUCATION | CREATIVE PAPERBACKS

I'M LARGE AND IN CHARGE!

table of contents

Published by Creative Education and Creative Paperbacks
P.O. Box 227, Mankato, Minnesota 56002
Creative Education and Creative Paperbacks
are imprints of The Creative Company
www.thecreativecompany.us

Design by Graham Morgan
Art direction by Blue Design (www.bluedes.com)

Images by Alamy/Joseph Sibilsky, 23; Dreamstime/Luis Viegas, 18–19, Marchello74, 14–15, Mechanik, cover (right), 24; Getty Images/Nerthuz, 3, 20–21; Unsplash/Caleb Ruiter, cover (left), 1, Esteban Zapata, cover (middle), 8–9, Ivan Bandura, 16, Jametlene Reskp, 17, Josiah Farrow, 2, Mitchell Luo, 6–7; Shutterstock/Michael Shake, 4, Troyan, 13, Rob Wilson 10–11

Library of Congress Cataloging-in-Publication Data
Names: Arnold, Quinn M., author.
Title: Big rigs / by Quinn M. Arnold.
Description: Mankato, Minnesota : Creative Education and Creative Paperbacks, [2025] | Series: Marvels | Includes bibliographical references and index. | Audience: Ages 4–7 | Audience: Grades K–1 | Summary: "An engine-revving introduction to big rigs, this transportation book for beginning readers features eye-catching photographs, humorous captions, and basic facts about the freight-carrying trucks. Includes a labeled vehicle guide, glossary, and further STEM resources"— Provided by publisher.
Identifiers: LCCN 2024014777 (print) | LCCN 2024014778 (ebook) | ISBN 9798889892250 (library binding) | ISBN 9781682775912 (paperback) | ISBN 9798889893363 (ebook)
Subjects: LCSH: Tractor trailer combinations--Juvenile literature. | Trucking—Juvenile literature. | CYAC: Tractor trailers. | Trucking. | LCGFT: Instructional and educational works.
Classification: LCC TL230.15 .A766 2025 (print) | LCC TL230.15 (ebook) | DDC 629.224—dc23/eng/20240425
LC record available at https://lccn.loc.gov/2024014777
LC ebook record available at https://lccn.loc.gov/2024014778

Printed in China

Big rigs are large trucks. They drive on **highways**. They carry heavy loads.

BUCKLE UP!
TRANS
ALIMENTOS

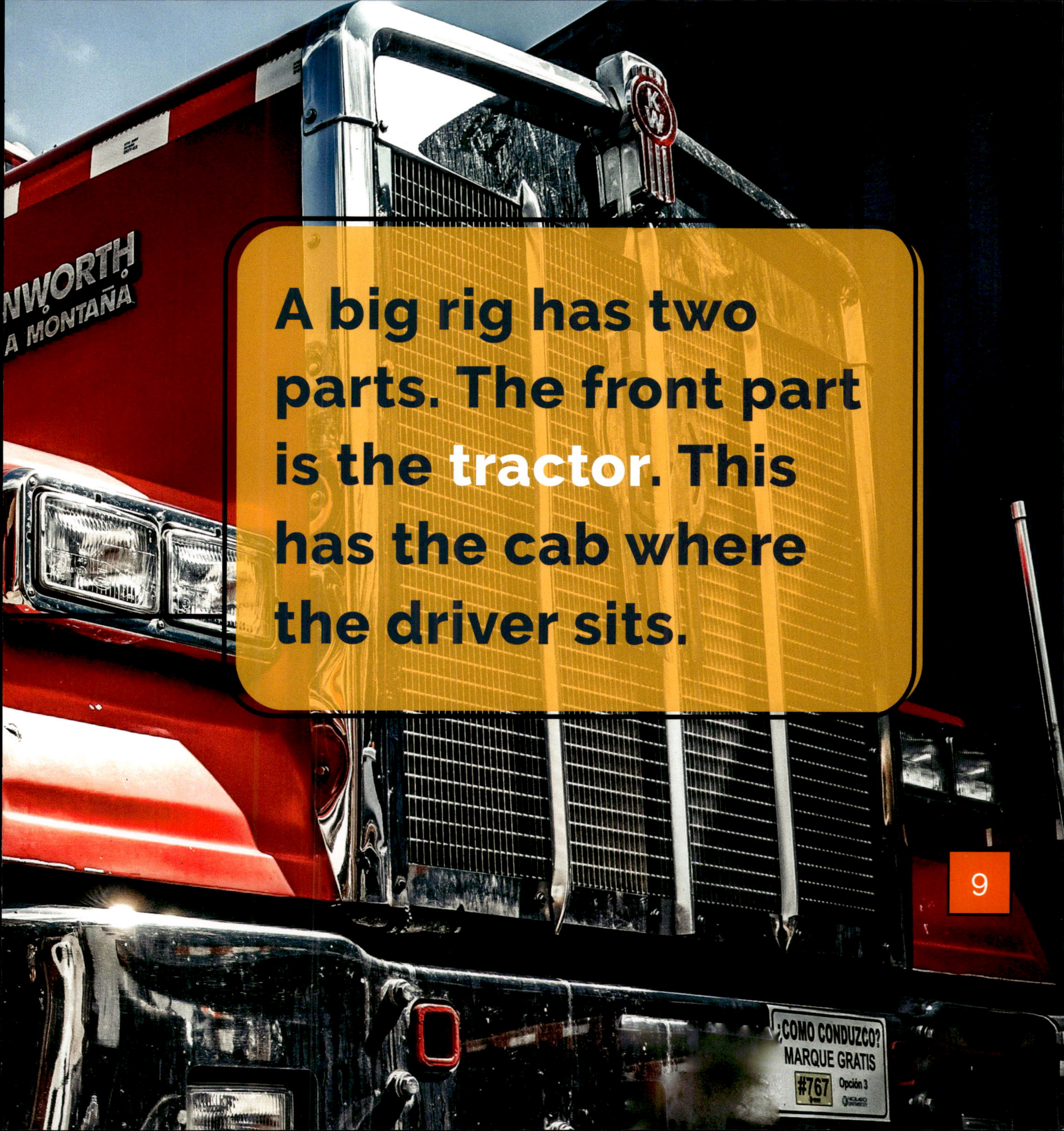

A big rig has two parts. The front part is the **tractor**. This has the cab where the driver sits.

The back of a big rig is the trailer. It is very long. The trailer carries the big rig's load.

Usually there is just one driver. But sometimes there are two. Two people can take turns driving.

ARE YOU SLEEPY?
NO. HUNGRY!

THIS LOAD IS TIED DOWN WITH RATCHET STRAPS.

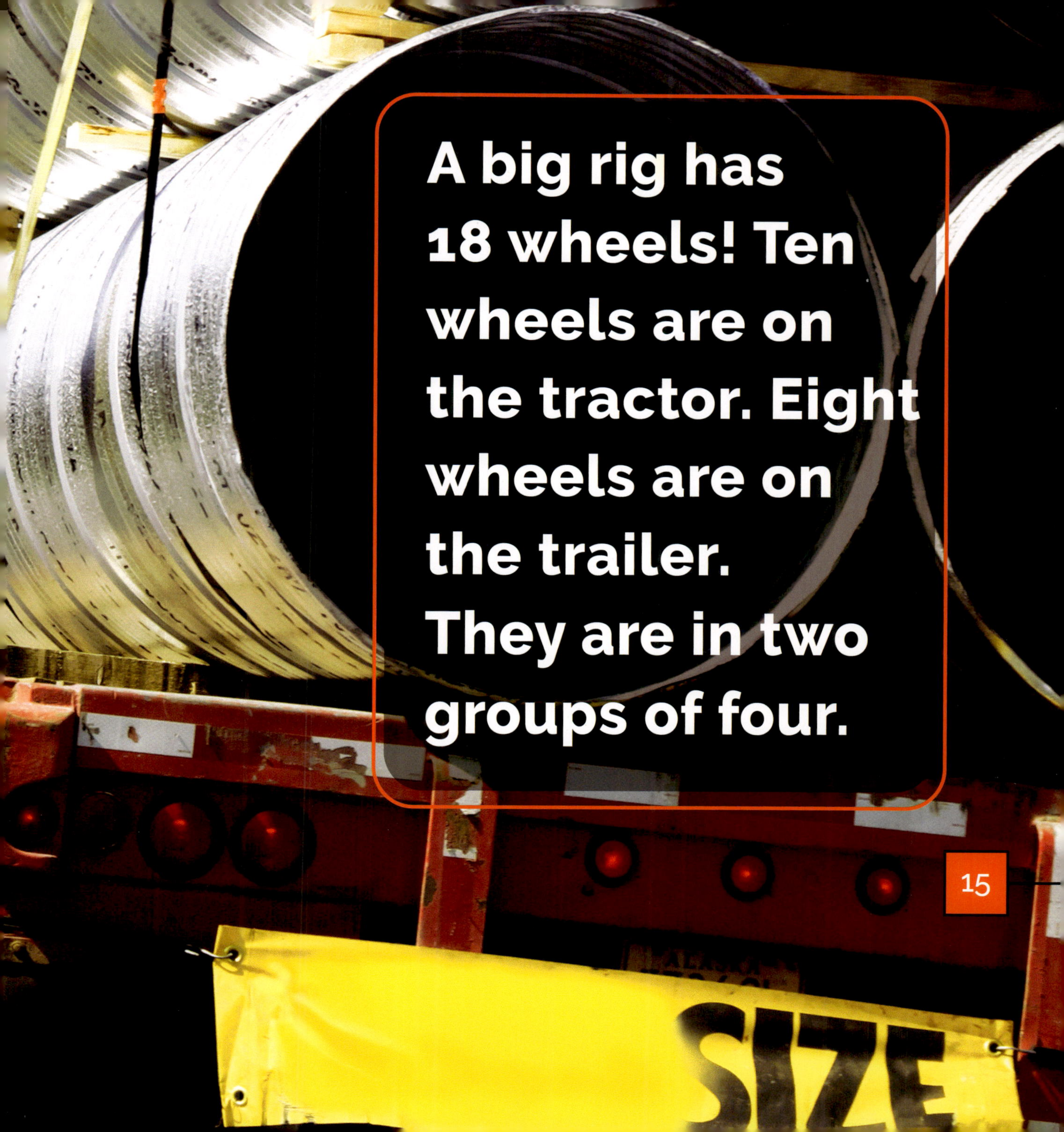

A big rig has 18 wheels! Ten wheels are on the tractor. Eight wheels are on the trailer. They are in two groups of four.

Big rigs haul **goods**. They drive from city to city.

LCI
EUROLOMA

PHEW. THAT WAS A LONG HAUL!

Farewell, big rigs!

[Picture a Big Rig]

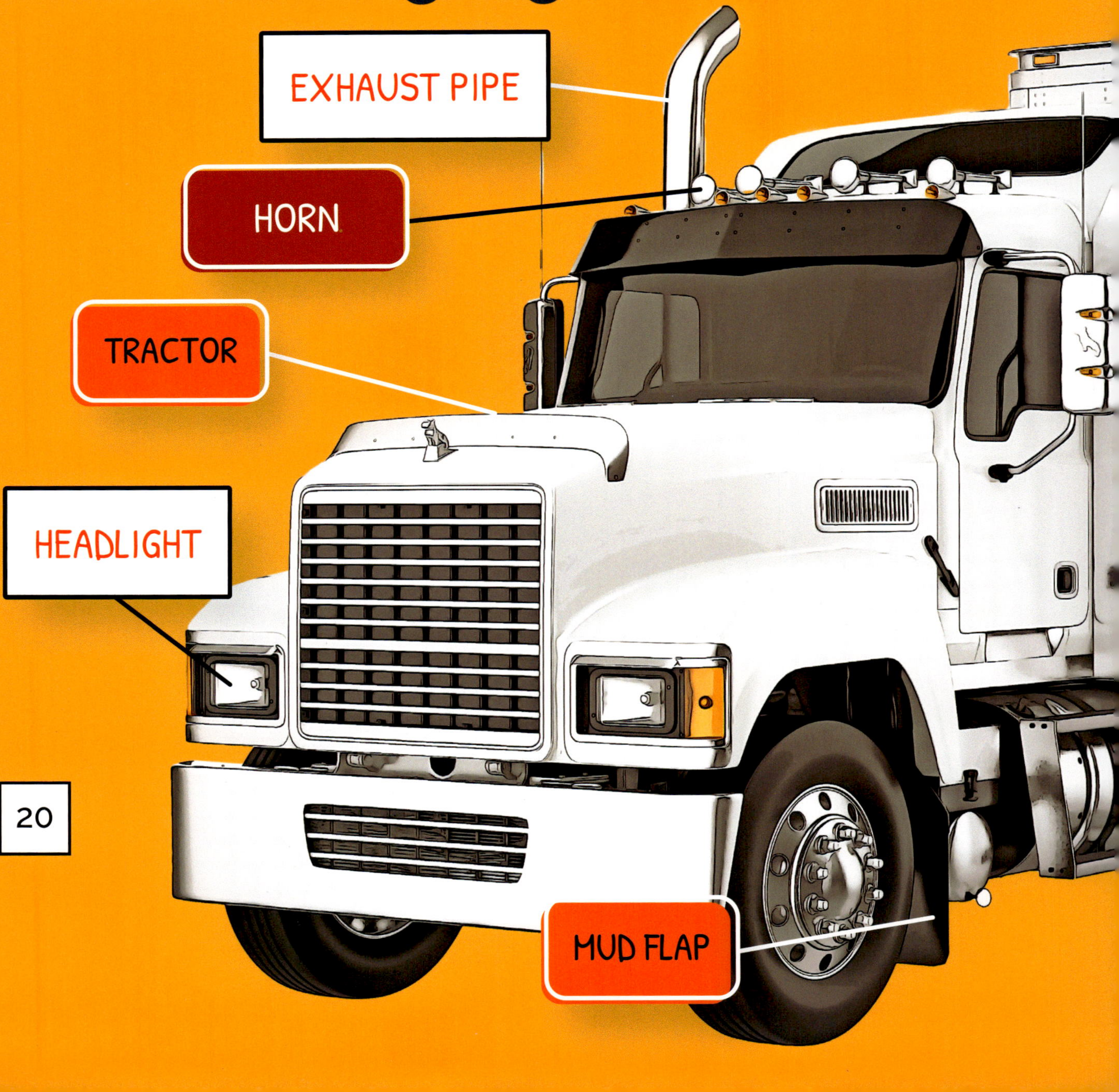

TRAILER
WHEEL

WORDS TO KNOW

goods: things people can buy in a store, such as food, electronics, or clothing

highway: the main road connecting cities

tractor: a short truck made up of a cab where the driver sits

READ MORE

Greve, Meg. *Big Rigs*. Mankato, Minn.: Creative Education and Creative Paperbacks, 2025.

Leed, Percy. *Look Inside a Big Rig: How it Works*. Minneapolis: Lerner Publications, 2024.

WEBSITES

Truck and Trucking
https://kids.britannica.com/students/article/truck-and-trucking/277434

An introduction to trucks, their history, and what they do today.

Truck Facts for Kids
https://kids.kiddle.co/Truck

Learn more about trucks and how they transport things from one place to another.

INDEX

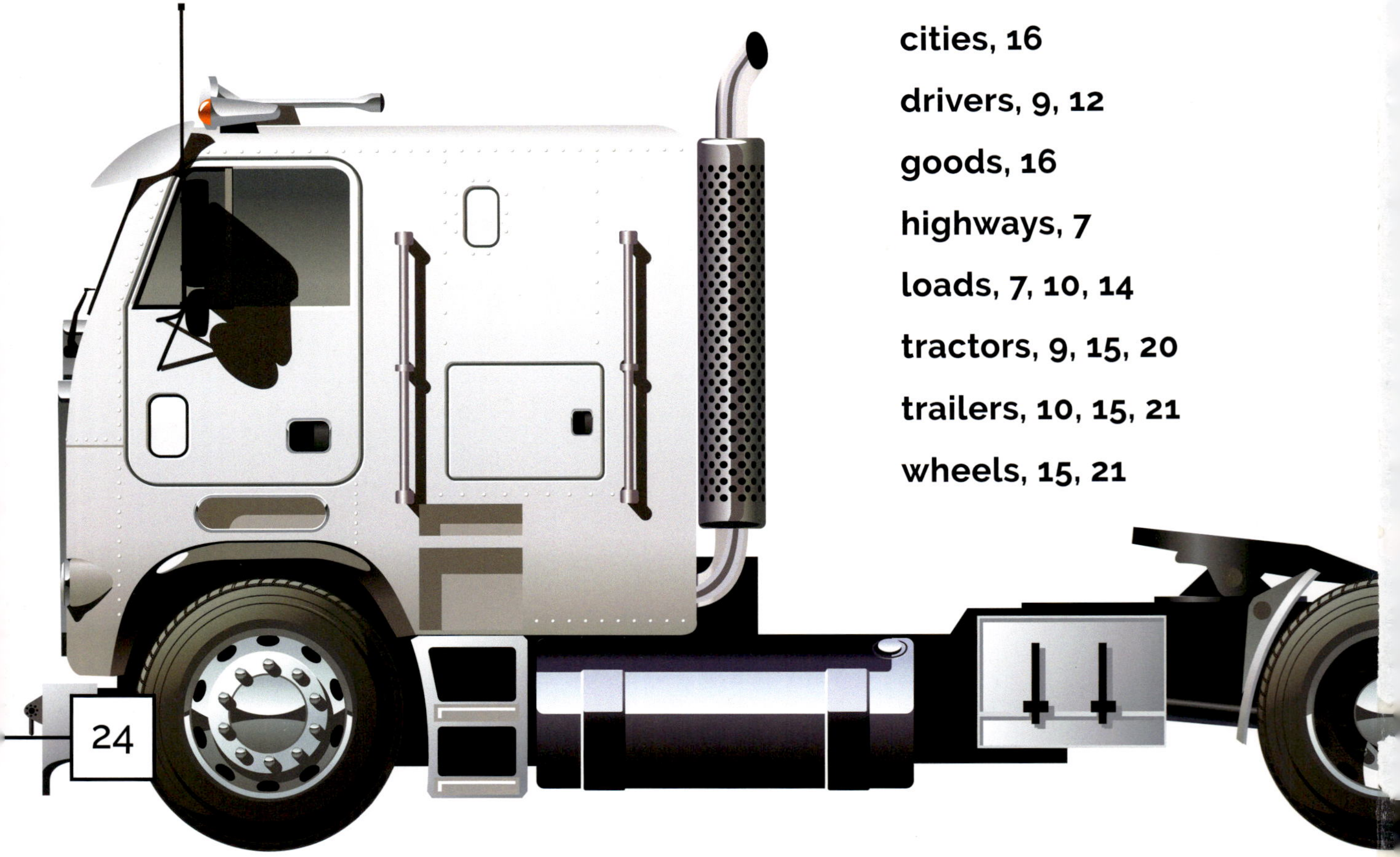